Documents for Democracy

Building America and Literacy Skills Through Primary Sources

Volume 3: 20th Century

**Prepared by
Veronica Burchard
Illustrations by Nicole M. Blank**

*Dedicated to my loving husband,
Kyle Burchard,
as well as my mentor and friend,
Claire McCaffery Griffin*

Unless otherwise noted, no part of this publication may be reproduced, stored, sourced off for use in other publications, or transmitted, in any form or by any means, electronic, mechanical, photocopying, recording or otherwise, without the prior written permission of the American Institute for History Education.

Edited by Matthew F. Galella
Design and typography by KJD Communications

Copyright © 2010 American Institute for History Education
All rights reserved

ISBN-13: 978-0-9826244-3-2

Printed in the United States of America
July 2010

Visit **www.aihe-bookstore.com**

Table of Contents

Theodore Roosevelt's Speech at the Minnesota State Fair 3
    Activating Prior Knowledge...................... 5
    Wrap-up Discussion Questions................ 14
    Teaching Suggestions............................... 15
    Graphic Organizer A................................ 16
    Handout B 17

Carrie Chapman Catt's Address to Congress 19
    Activating Prior Knowledge...................... 21
    Wrap-up Discussion Questions................ 30
    Teaching Suggestions............................... 31
    Graphic Organizer A................................ 32
    Handout B 33

Malcolm X's OAAU Founding Rally Address 35
    Activating Prior Knowledge...................... 37
    Wrap-up Discussion Questions................ 46
    Teaching Suggestions............................... 47
    Graphic Organizer A................................ 48
    Handout B 49

President Reagan's Challenger Disaster Address 51
    Activating Prior Knowledge...................... 53
    Wrap-up Discussion Questions................ 62
    Teaching Suggestions............................... 63
    Graphic Organizer A................................ 64
    Handout B 65

About the Author 67

Theodore Roosevelt's Speech at the Minnesota State Fair

We are a nation of pioneers and therefore our nation has in it more energy, more expansive power than any other in the wide world. To us is given the privilege of playing a leading part in the century that has just opened. A good many of you are probably acquainted with the old proverb: "Speak softly and carry a big stick—you will go far." If a man continually blusters, if he lacks civilty, a big stick will not save him from trouble; and neither will speaking softly avail, if back of the softness there does not lie strength, power. Let us make it evident that we intend to do justice. Then let us make it equally evident that we will not tolerate injustice being done to us in return. Let us further make it evident that we use no words which we are not prepared to back up with deeds, and that while our speech is always moderate, we are ready and willing to make it good. Such an attitude will be the surest possible guarantee of that self-respecting peace, the attainment of which is and must ever be the prime aim of a self-governing people.

Note to Teacher on Context:

The excerpted lines are taken from throughout Theodore Roosevelt's 4,000-plus word speech at the Minnesota State Fair.

Notes: _____

_____
_____
_____
_____
_____
_____
_____
_____
_____
_____
_____
_____
_____
_____
_____
_____
_____
_____
_____
_____
_____

Introduction

It was September 2, 1901. The 20th century had just begun. The vice president of the United States gazed at the happy crowd that had gathered at the Minnesota State Fair. Over the sounds of the livestock and children laughing, he began his speech.

Theodore Roosevelt

Theodore Roosevelt expressed his excitement and pride in America. Roosevelt believed the bold and strong spirit of America's pioneers would help America succeed in the new century. He saw chances for America to be powerful in the world.

He also spoke about an African proverb that meant a lot to him: "Speak softly and carry a big stick — you will go far." Roosevelt explained what the words meant to him. He believed people should say what they mean, and mean what they say. Nations, too, should be respectful to each other, but always be prepared to back up words with action.

Less than two weeks later, President William McKinley was assassinated, and Theodore Roosevelt became president. His "big stick" approach to other nations helped to grow America's navy, and America became more involved in world affairs in the 20th century.

What Is a Primary Source?

A primary source is a piece of history. It is an artifact from a time period, like a diary, a speech, a newspaper article, or a photograph. In this chapter, you will study *Theodore Roosevelt's Speech at the Minnesota State Fair* as a primary source from 1901, as a way to learn about that time period of American history.

_____
_____
_____
_____
_____
_____
_____

Activating Prior Knowledge:
Questions for Pre-Reading Discussion

1. What do you know about President Theodore Roosevelt? What do you associate with him?
2. Have you ever seen a picture of Mount Rushmore?
3. What do you know about the start of the 20th century?
4. How do you think people felt at the beginning of the new century?
5. How do you think your parents felt in the year 2001?
6. Have you heard the phrase "Speak softly and carry a big stick"? What do you think it means?

Vocabulary and Context Questions

Complete this page as you read. Using context clues and/or a dictionary, define each word:

Vocabulary

pioneers: *the first people to settle land*

expansive: *open and growing*

privilege: *honor*

acquainted: *familiar*

blusters: *yells, speaks rudely*

civility: *good manners*

avail: *success*

evident: *easy to understand*

tolerate: *to put up with*

moderate: *balanced*

attainment: *accomplishment*

prime: *first and most important*

Context Questions

1. Who delivered this speech? *Vice President Theodore Roosevelt*

2. When did he deliver it? *1901*

3. What was his purpose? *To express his thoughts on good personal and national policy*

4. Who listened to this speech? *People who had gathered at the Minnesota State Fair; other Americans*

Supplementary Information

- Theodore Roosevelt was born in New York in 1858.

- He was elected vice president under William McKinley in 1901; he served just six months in that office.

- Roosevelt expressed his belief that hard work done well was the most worthy pursuit for individuals, families, and nations. Roosevelt told the crowd, "You whom I am now addressing stand for the most part but one generation removed from these pioneers."

- Roosevelt favored the use of American military power to bring stability to other countries, including the Philippines, Cuba, and the Panama Canal Zone. He believed this kind of action (which his critics called imperialism) would improve America's place in the world.

Comprehension and Discussion Questions

- Who were the pioneers? *Individuals and families who were the first to settle the frontier. They faced many hardships with courage and a spirit of adventure.*

- Why do you think Roosevelt calls the United States a nation of pioneers? *Since the founding of America, individuals and families moved west across the continent. The spirit of America, Roosevelt believes, was found in these settlers who took on new challenges and adventures even at personal risk.*

- How does Roosevelt seem to feel about being an American?

We are a nation of pioneers and therefore our nation has in it more energy,
more expansive power than any other in the wide world.

He feels proud of being an American, and he believes America has great power to grow and expand.

Notes: _____
_____
_____
_____

To us is given the privilege of playing a leading part in the century that has just opened.

Supplementary Information

- The excerpted line in full reads, "It is because we believe with all our heart and soul in the greatness of this country, because we feel the thrill of hardy life in our veins, and are confident that to us is given the privilege of playing a leading part in the century that has just opened, that we hail with eager delight the opportunity to do whatever task Providence may allot us."

- Roosevelt explained the "leading part" the United States would play by comparing the United States to a husband. A husband's first duty is to his wife, but he also has an important public role to play in the community. A nation's first duty is to its own citizens, but it also has an important part to play on the world stage.

- Roosevelt saw these interactions with other nations as inevitable: "But we may be certain of one thing: whether we wish it or not, we cannot avoid hereafter having duties to do in the face of other nations. All that we can do is to settle whether we shall perform these duties well or ill."

Comprehension and Discussion Questions

- What does Roosevelt mean by "the century that has just opened"? *The 20th century*

- Does Roosevelt believe America has good times ahead or bad times ahead? *Good times. He is very optimistic.*

Notes:

_____
_____
_____
_____
_____
_____
_____
_____
_____
_____
_____
_____

Supplementary Information

- This was the first time Roosevelt used this famous phrase publicly. The first time he wrote the proverb was in a letter to Henry Sprague, which appears in the activities in this chapter on Page 15.

Comprehension and Discussion Questions

- How would you put this proverb in your own words? *Answers will vary. Students may suggest: Talk quietly, and have a weapon with you — you will do well. Or, be respectful, but be prepared to back up what you say — you will succeed.*
- What do you think about this proverb? Is it good advice? *Answers will vary.*

Notes: _____

A good many of you are probably acquainted with the old proverb: "Speak softly and carry a big stick — you will go far."

If a man continually blusters, if he lacks civility,
a big stick will not save him from trouble;
and neither will speaking softly avail,
if back of the softness there does not lie strength,
power.

Supplementary Information

- Roosevelt continued, "In private life there are few beings more obnoxious than the man who is always loudly boasting; and if the boaster is not prepared to back up his words his position becomes absolutely contemptible. So it is with the nation. It is both foolish and undignified to indulge in undue self-glorification, and, above all, in loose-tongued denunciation of other peoples. Whenever on any point we come in contact with a foreign power, I hope that we shall always strive to speak courteously and respectfully of that foreign power."

Comprehension and Discussion Questions

- Do you think Roosevelt valued good manners in his personal friendships? *Students likely will say yes.*

- Do you know people who say things but don't back up what they say with action? How does that make you feel? *Answers will vary.*

- Why does Roosevelt say both parts of the proverb are necessary? For example: What happens if you only speak softly, but have no big stick? *Words spoken rudely are not received well, whether you have a big stick or not. And the big stick brings force (or the threat of force) to the softly spoken words. According to Roosevelt, both are necessary for a person, or a nation, in order to be taken seriously.*

Notes: _____
_____
_____
_____
_____
_____
_____
_____
_____
_____
_____
_____
_____

Supplementary Information

- In his speech, Roosevelt referenced the Monroe Doctrine and said it should continue as the "cardinal feature" of U.S. foreign policy.

Comprehension and Discussion Questions

- What does Roosevelt believe the United States should make clear to other nations? *That the United States will do justice, and will not stand for injustice.*
- What do you think Roosevelt means by "justice"? How do you define this word? *Answers will vary.*
- Do you think America should follow this proverb today? Why or why not? *Answers will vary.*

Notes: _____
_____
_____
_____
_____
_____
_____
_____
_____
_____
_____
_____

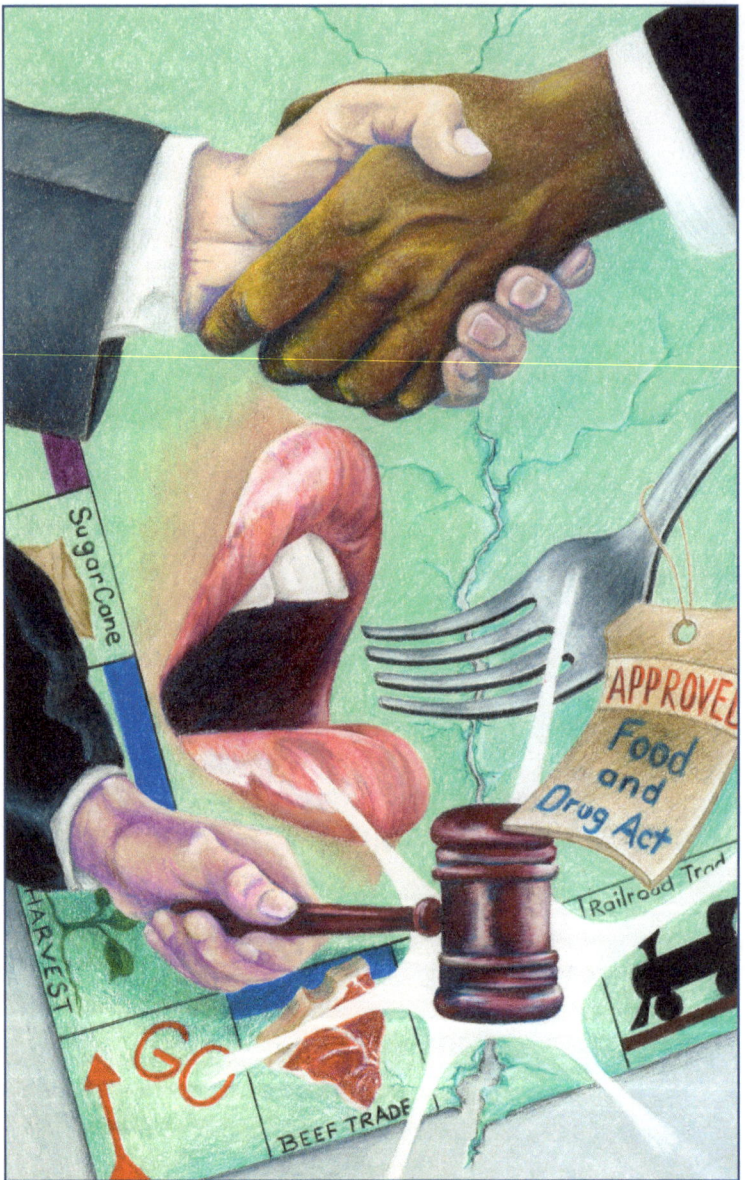

Let us make it evident that we intend to do justice. Then let us make it equally evident that we will not tolerate injustice being done to us in return.

_____
_____
_____
_____

We use no words which we are not prepared to back up with deeds, and while our speech is always moderate, we are ready and willing to make it good.

No nation capable of self-government, and of developing by its own efforts a sane and orderly civilization, no matter how small it may be, has anything to fear from us."

Comprehension and Discussion Questions

- What does Roosevelt mean by "make it good"? *Make good on it, or, back up what we saw with action or force. The United States should "walk the walk" and not just "talk the talk."*

- What happens when someone (a friend or even a coach or teacher) says something but then does not back up his or her words with action? Are you more or less likely to believe them? *Students may point out that actions speak louder than words. When someone says one thing but does not back up their words with actions, their sincerity and credibility are called into question.*

- How can you personally act out this principle? *Choosing words carefully, not making promises one cannot keep, always standing by one's statements.*

Notes: _____

Supplementary Information

- Roosevelt saw it as a source of pride that the U.S. military had been used to build up nations. "Throughout a large part of our national career our history has been one of expansion, the expansion being of different kinds at different times. This expansion is not a matter of regret, but of pride. It is vain to tell a people as masterful as ours that the spirit of enterprise is not safe. The true American has never feared to run risks when the prize to be won was of sufficient value.

Supplementary Information

- Roosevelt won the Nobel Peace Prize in 1906 for negotiating peace in the Russo-Japanese War. He was the first American to win the prize.

Comprehension and Discussion Questions

- What does Roosevelt claim the attitude of the proverb will bring for America? *A self-respecting peace.*

- Why do you think Roosevelt says "self-respecting peace" and not simply "peace"? *A nation may be able to live in peace while ignoring injustice. For Roosevelt, this would not be an acceptable compromise.*

- Do you think Roosevelt is right? Explain. *Answers will vary.*

- Can you apply Roosevelt advice to your own life? How? *Students may suggest dealing with bullies on the playground or ball field; earning their parents trust; doing well in school by following through on assignments; achievement in sports by following through on practices and games.*

Notes: _____

Such an attitude will be the surest possible guarantee of that self-respecting peace, the attainment of which is and must ever be the prime aim of a self-governing people.

Theodore Roosevelt's Speech at the Minnesota State Fair

We are a nation of pioneers and therefore our nation has in it more energy,

more expansive power than any other in the wide world.

To us is given the privilege of playing a leading part in the century that has just opened.

A good many of you are probably acquainted with the old proverb: "Speak softly and carry a big stick — you will go far."

If a man continually blusters, if he lacks civility, a big stick will not save him from trouble; and neither will speaking softly avail, if back of the softness there does not lie strength, power.

Let us make it evident that we intend to do justice. Then let us make it equally evident that we will not tolerate injustice being done to us in return.

Let us further make it evident that we use no words which we are not prepared to back up with deeds, and that while our speech is always moderate, we are ready and willing to make it good.

Such an attitude will be the surest possible guarantee of that self-respecting peace, the attainment of which is and must ever be the prime aim of a self-governing people.

Name: _____   Date: _____

Wrap-up Discussion Questions

- Do you think Theodore Roosevelt would make a good friend? Or older brother?

- Roosevelt had six children. What kind of father do you think he was? What kinds of lessons do you think he thought were most important to teach his children?

- How can people figure out what their gift is?

- How can you "speak softly and carry a big stick" in your own life?

Teaching Suggestions

Activity I: Close Reading

Divide the class into pairs or trios and give each group a slip of paper with an excerpt from *Theodore Roosevelt's Speech at the Minnesota State Fair* (**Graphic Organizer A**). Have them put the sentence(s) in their own words. After a few moments, reconvene the class and distribute complete copies of **Handout A** to each student. Have groups read their paraphrases in turn, and discuss each as a class and decide if it is a faithful and complete paraphrase. Have students complete the chart on **Handout A** with the class paraphrases. When all slips are completed, read the original version of *Theodore Roosevelt's Speech at the Minnesota State Fair* aloud and discuss how the class version compared with the original.

Activity II: Compare/Contrast

Have students interview their parents about what it was like during the turn of the 21st century. Encourage them to ask about what they thought the new century would hold for them, personally as well as for the United States. Then have students create a Venn diagram with two circles: a) President Roosevelt — 1900 and b) My parents — 2000. Have them fill in information about the two historic periods using information from Roosevelt's speech, and from the interviews. If students are old enough, they can add information to the Venn diagram based on their own experiences, too!

Activity III: Creative Writing

1. Have students imagine they were in attendance at the Minnesota State Fair in 1901. Ask them to write a fictional letter to a friend living in another part of the United States, explaining what Roosevelt said in his speech and how it made them feel.

2. Have students write a short journal entry about a time in their life when they "spoke softly and carried a big stick." For example, it could be a time when they conducted themselves respectfully and made it clear they would back up their words with action. How did others react? How did it make them feel about themselves?

Activity IV: Application

Have students read a short excerpt from the letter to Henry Sprague on **Handout B** in which Theodore Roosevelt first referenced the African proverb, and answer the questions that follow. The actual letter can be viewed at **http://www.loc.gov/exhibits/treasures/trm139.html**

Name: _____ Date: _____

Graphic Organizer A

We are a nation of pioneers and therefore our nation has in it more energy, more power than any other in the wide world.	*Put this passage in your own words:*
To us is given the privilege of playing a leading part in the century that has just opened.	*Put this passage in your own words:*
A good many of you are probably acquainted with the old proverb: "Speak softly and carry a big stick — you will go far."	*Put this passage in your own words:*
If a man continually blusters, if he lacks civility, a big stick will not save him from trouble; and neither will speaking softly avail, if back of the softness there does not lie strength, power;	*Put this passage in your own words:*
Let us make it evident that we intend to do justice. Then let us make it equally evident that we will not tolerate injustice being done to us in return.	*Put this passage in your own words:*
We use no words which we are not prepared to back up with deeds, and while our speech is always moderate, we are ready and willing to make it good.	*Put this passage in your own words:*
Such an attitude will be the surest possible guarantee of that self-respecting peace, the attainment of which is and must ever be the prime aim of a self-governing people.	*Put this passage in your own words:*

Name: _____ Date: _____

Handout B: Roosevelt's Letter to Henry Sprague

Directions: *Read the lines from Roosevelt's letter below. At the time he wrote this, Roosevelt was governor of New York. In this letter, he tells his friend Henry Sprague (whom he addressed as Harry in the greeting) about how he was able to win a political fight against the Republicans in the state.*

Dear Harry,
I have always been fond of the West African proverb: "Speak softly and carry a big stick; you will go far."
If I had not carried the big stick, the organization would not have gotten behind me,
and if I had yelled and blustered ... I would not have had ten votes.
But I was entirely good humored,
kept perfectly cool ...

1. How does Roosevelt describe his actions?

2. What do you think "Speak softly and carry a big stick" means here?

Carrie Chapman Catt's Address to Congress

Woman suffrage is inevitable. Three distinct causes made it inevitable. First, the history of our country. Ours is a nation born of revolution, of rebellion. Second, the suffrage for women already established in the United States makes women suffrage for the nation inevitable. No one will deny it. The only question left is when and how will it be completely established. Third, the leadership of the United States in the world democracy compels the enfranchisement of its own women. Your party platforms have pledged women suffrage. Then why not be honest, why not put the amendment through Congress? We shall have a happier nation, we women will be free to support loyally the party of our choice, and we shall be far prouder of our history. The time for woman suffrage has come. The woman's hour has struck. Holding her torch aloft, liberty is pointing the way onward and upward and saying to America, "Come." Woman suffrage is coming—you know it. Will you help or hinder it?

Note to Teacher on Context:

The first and final lines of Carrie Chapman Catt's speech are preserved here, and main ideas from each section are also excerpted.

Notes: _____

Introduction

Carrie Chapman Catt

The Constitution did not protect a woman's right to vote when it was first written. Only white men had this right. The Fifteenth Amendment gave black men the right to vote, but as of 1917, women still did not have a say in choosing America's leaders or what kinds of laws were passed. The United States was based on the people governing themselves. But women had no voice in government.

Beginning in the mid 1800s, women across America had been talking with each other, having meetings, and forming groups to try to win the vote for female citizens of the United States. One of these groups was called the National American Woman Suffrage Association (NAWSA). Carrie Chapman Catt was the president of NAWSA.

By the end of the 1800s, some states had given women the right to vote. But Catt believed that for women to be able to vote everywhere, an amendment to the federal Constitution was needed. She went before Congress in 1917 and gave an important speech. She asked the senators and representatives from all the states to make a choice. Would they support votes for women, or work against them?

What Is a Primary Source?

A primary source is a piece of history. It is an artifact from a time period, like a diary, a speech, a newspaper article, or a photograph. In this chapter, you will study the speech *Carrie Chapman Catt's Address to Congress* as a primary source from 1917, as a way to learn about that time period of American history.

Activating Prior Knowledge: Questions for Pre-Reading Discussion

1. Did you know that American women did not have the right to vote until the Nineteenth Amendment was ratified in 1920?
2. Have you ever heard of women's suffragists? What do you know about them?
3. Why is voting important in the United States?
4. Why do you think women wanted the right to vote?
5. What kinds of things do you think Carrie Chapman Catt said to members of Congress (who were all men except for one congresswoman) about votes for women?

Vocabulary and Context Questions

Complete this page as you read. Using context clues and/or a dictionary, define each word:

Vocabulary

suffrage: *the right to vote*

inevitable: *certain or unavoidable*

distinct: *individual*

revolution: *complete change in rulers*

rebellion: *fighting against those in power*

deny: *say something is not true*

compel: *to force something to happen*

enfranchisement: *giving full rights of citizenship, especially voting rights*

pledged: *promised*

hinder: *make something more difficult*

Context Questions

1. Who delivered this speech? *Carrie Chapman Catt*

2. When did she deliver it? *1917*

3. What was her purpose? *To win support for a constitutional amendment providing women with the right to vote*

4. Who listened to this speech? *Members of Congress, American citizens, citizens of other countries*

Supplementary Information

- Carrie Chapman Catt was born in Ripon, Wisconsin, in 1859.
- She was a close colleague of suffragist and civil rights leader Susan B. Anthony.
- Catt served as president of NAWSA from 1900 until 1904; she was elected a second time in 1915 and served until 1920, the year the Nineteenth Amendment was ratified.

Comprehension and Discussion Questions

- What does "inevitable" mean? *Definitely going to happen, no matter what.*
- How many causes does Catt say have made women's votes certain in the future? *Three.*
- Why do you think Catt starts out by telling Congress that women will definitely win the right to vote? *It may make them curious to know why she believes that; they may want to be part of a movement that is certain to succeed. It may also make them believe it is pointless to fight against something that is definitely going to happen.*

Notes: _____
_____
_____
_____
_____
_____
_____
_____

Woman suffrage is inevitable.
Three distinct causes made it inevitable.

First, the history of our country.
Ours is a nation born of revolution, of rebellion.

Supplementary Information

- Catt explains in this part of her speech, "The American Revolutionists boldly proclaimed the heresies: 'Taxation without representation is tyranny.' 'Governments derive their just powers from the consent of the governed.' The colonists won, and the nation which was established ... has held unfailingly that these two fundamental principles of democratic government are ... the sheet anchor of our liberties."

- Catt referenced Abraham Lincoln's *Gettysburg Address* as an example of the American commitment to government by the people and for the people, as well as Woodrow Wilson's words about World War I: "We are fighting for the things which we have always carried nearest to our hearts: for democracy, for the right of those who submit to authority to have a voice in their own government."

Comprehension and Discussion Questions

- What does Catt mean when she says the United States was born of rebellion? *The colonies rebelled against the tyranny of the British king and declared independence from England.*

- Why does Catt compare women's suffragists to the rebelling colonists of 1776? *Both were fighting for a voice in their own government.*

Notes: _____
_____
_____
_____
_____
_____
_____
_____
_____
_____
_____
_____
_____
_____
_____
_____

Supplementary Information

- In 1917, several states had amended their own constitutions to allow women to vote. The federal Constitution, however, had no guarantee of voting rights for women.

- Wyoming became the first state to allow women to vote in 1890. Colorado, Idaho, and Utah followed. Several other states amended their constitutions to allow limited suffrage.

- Catt elaborated, "Do you realize that in no other country in the world with democratic tendencies is suffrage so completely denied as in a considerable number of our own states? There are thirteen black states where no suffrage for women exists, and fourteen others where suffrage for women is more limited than in many foreign countries."

- In the late 19th century, another organization, the American Woman Suffrage Association (AWSA), had advocated working for women's votes on the state level. AWSA merged with what was then called the National Woman Suffrage Association to form NAWSA. As president of NAWSA, Catt promoted what she called the "winning plan" to work for voting rights on the state and federal levels.

Comprehension and Discussion Questions

- Why does Catt say suffrage for women has already been established in parts of the United States? *In 1917, some states had given women some rights to vote. But they still could not vote in most states.*

Second, the suffrage for women already established in the United States makes women suffrage for the nation inevitable. No one will deny it. The only question left is when and how will it be completely established.

- Do you think Catt makes a good argument here? If you were a congressman, would you believe her? Why or why not? *Answers will vary.*

Notes: _____

_____

Third, the leadership of the United States in world democracy compels the enfranchisement of its own women.

Comprehension and Discussion Questions

- What is the third reason Catt gives for why women will definitely win the right to vote? *The United States is a leader for other countries and should always set a good example for what democracy means.*

- Why does Catt believe a democratic nation must allow women to vote? *A so-called democracy cannot be a true democracy if half the citizens are not allowed to have a voice in government.*

Notes: _____

Supplementary Information

- Catt also argued the principles of the *Declaration of Independence* call for equal voting rights. Further, those principles have been cited by oppressed people worldwide: "The maxims of the *Declaration* are now called 'American principles' … They have become the slogans of every movement toward liberty the world around. Not a people, race, or class striving for freedom is there anywhere in the world that has not made our axioms the chief weapon of the struggle."

Supplementary Information

- Catt hints that women voters will be in a position to re-elect leaders who fight for women's votes, as well as to vote against leaders who opposed women's suffrage. "Every delay, every trick, every political dishonesty from now on will antagonize the women of the land more and more, and when the party or parties which have so delayed woman suffrage finally let it come, their sincerity will be doubted and their appeal to the new voters will be met with suspicion. This is the psychology of the situation. Can you afford the risk? Think it over."

Comprehension and Discussion Questions

- What does Catt mean by "an amendment"? *An amendment to the Constitution that would grant women in all states the right to vote.*

- If women win the right to vote, they will one day be voting for (or against) the members of Congress Catt is addressing in this speech. Does this help you understand why she tells them that women's suffrage is "inevitable" (or definitely going to happen)? *Catt is hinting that congressmen who support a constitutional amendment will be more likely to be re-elected once women have the right to vote.*

Notes: _____

Your party platforms have pledged women suffrage. Then why not be honest, why not put the amendment through Congress? We shall have a happier nation, we women will be free to support loyally the party of our choice, and we shall be far prouder of our history.

The time for woman suffrage has come.
The woman's hour has struck.

- Catt uses words like "hour has struck." These words make you think of what things? *Time, or a clock.*
- Why do you think Catt uses these words? Are they a good way of getting her ideas across? *Using words like "time," and "woman's hour" show how the passage of time is leading to women's winning of the vote. The image may also bring to mind how much time has passed in the years since America was founded on the basis that all men are created equal. Finally, time's march is inexorable — this metaphor is a continuation of her argument that women's suffrage is inevitable; that is, it is as impossible to stop as it would be impossible to stop time.*

Notes: _____

_____
_____
_____
_____
_____
_____
_____
_____
_____
_____
_____
_____
_____
_____
_____
_____

Supplementary Information

- Catt intoned, "There is one thing mightier than kings and armies" — aye, than Congresses and political parties — "the power of an idea when its time has come to move."

Comprehension and Discussion Questions

- What does Catt mean by "The woman's hour has struck"? *It's time for woman to have a say in her own political destiny, to have a vote.*

Supplementary Information

- The Nineteenth Amendment was ratified in 1920, three years after Catt's address.
- After the passage of the Nineteenth Amendment, Catt retired from NAWSA and founded the League of Women Voters — an organization that is still active today.

Comprehension and Discussion Questions

- What does "liberty" holding a torch make you think of? *The Statue of Liberty.*
- Why do you think Catt chooses to describe Lady Liberty? *The Statue of Liberty is a symbol of America. The symbol for liberty is a woman, and this is especially meaningful since Catt is trying to win the right to vote for women. Self-government is essential for liberty.*
- Why do you think Catt ends her speech by asking members of Congress if they will help or hinder (try to stop) women from winning the right to vote? *It reminds them that all Americans will be watching how they respond to women suffragists.*

Notes: _____
_____
_____
_____
_____
_____
_____
_____

Holding her torch aloft, liberty is pointing the way onward and upward and saying to America, "Come." Woman suffrage is coming — you know it. Will you help or hinder it?

Carrie Chapman Catt's Address to Congress

Woman suffrage is inevitable.
Three distinct causes made it inevitable.

First, the history of our country. Ours is a nation born of revolution, of rebellion.

Second, the suffrage for women already established in the United States makes women suffrage for the nation inevitable. No one will deny it. The only question left is when and how will it be completely established.

Third, the leadership of the United States in world democracy compels the enfranchisement of its own women.

Your party platforms have pledged women suffrage. Then why not be honest, why not put the amendment through Congress?

We shall have a happier nation, we women will be free to support loyally the party of our choice, and we shall be far prouder of our history.

The time for woman suffrage has come.
The woman's hour has struck.

Holding her torch aloft, liberty is pointing the way onward and upward and saying to America, "Come." Woman suffrage is coming — you know it. Will you help or hinder it?

Name: _____ Date: _____

Wrap-up Discussion Questions

- How do you think members of Congress reacted to Catt's speech?

- How do you think congressmen from states where women had the right to vote responded to the speech, compared with congressmen from states where women could not vote?

- What does Catt want congressmen to believe about women's suffrage?

- What personal qualities does Catt seem to reveal about herself?

Teaching Suggestions

Activity I: Close Reading

Separate the class into pairs or trios and give each group a slip with an excerpt from *Carrie Chapman Catt's Address to Congress* (**Graphic Organizer A**). Have them put the sentence(s) in their own words. After a few moments, reconvene the class and distribute complete copies of **Handout A** to each student. Have groups read their paraphrases in turn, and discuss each as a class and decide if it is a faithful and complete paraphrase. Have students complete the chart on **Handout A** with the class paraphrases. When all slips are completed, read the original version of *Carrie Chapman Catt's Address to Congress* aloud and discuss how the class version compared with the original.

Activity II: Compare and Contrast

Have students make a list of the personal qualities or character traits Carrie Chapman Catt demonstrates in her speech. For example, you might suggest "courageous, fearless, bold, stern, knowledgeable, non-violent, polite," and others. (Students may also suggest that Catt did not go far enough, and did not make a strong enough case.) Then have students select another civil or political rights leader they have learned about and create a Venn diagram comparing and contrasting the character traits exemplified by Catt and the individual selected.

Activity III: Creative Writing

1. Have students imagine they are Carrie Chapman Catt, and they have received a letter from another woman's suffrage leader, Alice Paul. She lives in Washington, D.C., and knows of Catt's speech, but believes it was too meek and mild to make any real difference. How would Catt respond? Have students assume the persona of Catt and write a one-paragraph letter to Paul explaining why she gave the speech the way she did and what she hoped to accomplish from it.

2. Ask students to think about the word "inevitable" and discuss its definition. Divide students into pairs or trios and have them identify an activity that they are not currently able to do, but they feel will be inevitable later in life. (For example, drive a car, stay out late with friends, get a job, go to college, etc.) Have them write a speech to a parent or teacher, attempting to convince them of the inevitability of the activity and perhaps make a case that they should be able to do it now because it is inevitable.

Activity III: Application

1. Ask students to imagine they have been hired by Carrie Chapman Catt to create a flier and a logo for NAWSA and the women's suffrage movement. Catt would like the key points of her speech included in the flier, and the logo should be featured prominently on the flier as well. Have students create fliers on poster-board or large paper.

2. Have students learn about the National Woman's Party (NWP) and their activities during 1917 — the time of Catt's speech. Have them present what they learned in a short oral report. After the class has reported, conduct a large group discussion to answer this question: Which do you think was more effective, the less radical tactics of NAWSA, or the more militant ones of NWP?

3. Have students research the history of voting rights for women in their own state, and present what they have learned in a short oral report or poster-board presentation. They can use **Handout B** as a guide in their research.

Name: _____ Date: _____

Graphic Organizer A

Woman suffrage is inevitable. Three distinct causes made it inevitable.	*Put this passage in your own words:*
First, the history of our country. Ours is a nation born of revolution, of rebellion.	*Put this passage in your own words:*
Second, the suffrage for women already established in the United States makes women suffrage for the nation inevitable. No one will deny it. The only question left is when and how will it be completely established.	*Put this passage in your own words:*
Third, the leadership of the United States in world democracy compels the enfranchisement of its own women.	*Put this passage in your own words:*
Your party platforms have pledged women suffrage. Then why not be honest, why not put the amendment through Congress? We shall have a happier nation, we women will be free to support loyally the party of our choice, and we shall be far prouder of our history.	*Put this passage in your own words:*
The time for woman suffrage has come. The woman's hour has struck.	*Put this passage in your own words:*
Holding her torch aloft, liberty is pointing the way onward and upward and saying to America, "Come." Woman suffrage is coming — you know it. Will you help or hinder it?	*Put this passage in your own words:*

Name: _____   Date: _____

Handout B:

Votes for women in _____ (my state)

Directions: *As you research the history of women's suffrage in your state, think about the following questions:*

1. When did _____ grant women the right to vote?
2. Did women have any voting rights before the Nineteenth Amendment was passed?
3. Were any women's suffrage conventions, parades or demonstrations held in _____?
4. Did any well-known historical figures campaign in your state?
5. What methods did women suffragists use in _____ to bring attention to their cause?
6. Who were the senators and representatives from _____ when the Nineteenth Amendment was passed? What was their point of view on votes for women?

Malcolm X

OAAU Founding Rally Address

We have formed an organization known as the Organization of Afro-American Unity.

We want freedom by any means necessary. We want justice by any means necessary. We want equality by any means necessary.

We don't think that we should have to sit around and wait for some segregationist congressmen and senators and a President from Texas in Washington, D.C, to make up their minds that our people are due now some degree of civil rights. No, we want it now or we don't think anybody should have it.

When we say Afro-American, we include everyone in the Western Hemishphere of African descent. So the purpose of the Organization of Afro-American Unity is to unite everyone in the Western Hemisphere of African descent into one united froce. And then, we will unite with our brothers on the motherland, on the continent of Africa.

We must unite together in order to go forwrd together. Africa will not go forward any faster than we will and we will not go forward any faster than Africa will. We have one destiny and we've had one past.

Note to Teacher on Context:

Malcolm X's address began, "As many of you know, last March when it was announced that I was no longer in the Black Muslim movement, it was pointed out that it was my intention to work among the 22 million non-Muslim Afro-Americans and to try and form some type of organization, or create a situation where the young people, our young people, the students and others could study the problems of our people for a period of time and then come up with a new ... There have been many of our people ... who have taken it upon themselves to try and pool their ideas and to come up with some kind of solution to the problem that confronts all of our people. And tonight we are here to try and get an understanding of what it is they've come up with. ... "

Notes: _____

Introduction

Malcolm X

The Civil War ended in 1865. The Constitution was amended to say the government must treat all people equally under the law. Even so, African Americans faced discrimination after the Civil War through to the 20th century.

Famous civil rights leaders like Martin Luther King Jr. preached nonviolent protest as a way of fighting racism. Civil rights leader Malcolm X saw things differently. Malcolm X believed that nonviolence would not win over violent racism. He believed African Americans should unite and fight back against racist whites. He even thought African Americans should separate from whites and form their own independent communities.

Malcolm X had once belonged to the Nation of Islam. He left the Nation of Islam so he could work to unite all people of African descent, of all religions. He helped form the Organization of Afro-American Unity, or OAAU. He spoke at its founding rally in 1964. He talked about his belief that African Americans shared the same destiny as their brothers and sisters in Africa.

What Is a Primary Source?

A primary source is a piece of history. It is an artifact from a time period, like a diary, a speech, a newspaper article, or a photograph. In this chapter, you will study *Malcolm X's OAAU Founding Rally Address* as a primary source from 1964, as a way to learn about that time period of American history.

Activating Prior Knowledge:
Questions for Pre-Reading Discussion

1. Have you ever heard of the Civil Rights Movement? When did it take place? What do you know about it?
2. Have you ever heard the names Martin Luther King Jr., Rosa Parks, or Malcolm X? Who were they?
3. Do you know what the word "segregation" means?
4. If you were asked to describe a perfect America in three words, what words would you use?
5. Have you heard the phrase "The ends justify the means"? What do you think it means?
6. Do you belong to any clubs at school? Do you play on a team, or belong to any other organizations outside of school like 4-H, or Boy Scouts or Girl Scouts?
7. Why do people like to form and join clubs?

Vocabulary and Context Questions

Complete this page as you read. Using context clues and/or a dictionary, define each word:

Vocabulary

unity: oneness, *togetherness*

means: *methods*

justice: *fairness*

equality: *legal equality*

segregationist: *one who supports segregation (the forced segregation of races)*

descent: *heritage*

destiny: *fate, future*

Context Questions

1. Who delivered this speech? *Malcolm X*
2. When did he deliver it? *1964*
3. What was his purpose? *To explain the purpose of the Organization of Afro-American Unity*
4. Who listened to this speech? *People who had gathered at the OAAU Founding Rally*

Supplementary Information

- Malcolm Little was born in Omaha, Nebraska, in 1925. He changed his name to Malcolm X in 1952 after joining the Nation of Islam a few years earlier.

- Malcolm X explained why he was working to form the OAAU. He said, "I was blessed to make a religious pilgrimage to the holy city of Mecca where I met many people from all over the world, and I realized that our African brothers have gained their independence faster than you and I here in America have. My traveling was designed to help to find out how. Despite their differences, [our brothers in Africa] were able to sit down and form what was known as the Organization of African Unity, which has formed a coalition and is working in conjunction with each other to fight a common enemy."

- He referred to the Organization of African Unity as "working … to fight a common enemy." Fighting this common enemy also would be the work of the OAAU, modeled after the OAU.

- He went on, "The Organization of Afro-American Unity, organized and structured by a cross section of the Afro-American people living in the United States of America, has been patterned after the letter and spirit of the Organization of African Unity which was established at Addis Ababa, Ethiopia, in May of 1963."

Comprehension and Discussion Questions

- What organization does Malcolm X say has been formed? *An Organization of Afro-American Unity.*

We have formed an organization known as the Organization of Afro-American Unity.

30

- What kind of organization do you think this might be? *Students may suggest it is a group to help bring African Americans together.*

Notes: _____

_____

_____

_____

We want freedom by any means necessary.

Comprehension and Discussion Questions

- What does Malcolm X say he and his fellow Afro-Americans want? *Freedom.*

- Do you know any ways that African Americans were not free during this time? *Into the 1960s many states enforced laws requiring segregation of races. Blacks were not allowed to use many of the same public facilities as whites.*

Notes: _____
_____
_____
_____
_____
_____
_____
_____
_____
_____
_____
_____
_____
_____
_____
_____
_____
_____
_____
_____
_____

Supplementary Information

- Malcolm X specifically rejected other civil rights leaders' calls for nonviolent resistance. He often used the words "by any means necessary" to communicate the difference in approach between himself and other leaders.

- One of Malcolm X's colleagues said this about the OAAU: "We agreed on self-reliance, about what people would have to do, and that an ethnic community was really a small nation … "

Supplementary Information

- The OAAU resolved, "We assert that in those areas where the government is either unable or unwilling to protect the lives and property of our people, that our people are within our rights to protect themselves by whatever means necessary."

- Malcolm X questioned the sincerity of white Americans early in this speech. "You and I live in a country which is supposed to be the citadel of education, freedom, justice, democracy, and all of those other pretty-sounding words."

Comprehension and Discussion Questions

- What does Malcolm X say the OAAU wants in these lines? *Freedom and justice.*

- Why do you think he keeps repeating "by any means necessary"? *Students may suggest he wants people to remember that point. They may say Malcolm X wants to get across that he will do whatever he has to do in order to win justice and equality for African Americans.*

Notes: _____

We want justice by any means necessary.
We want equality by any means necessary.

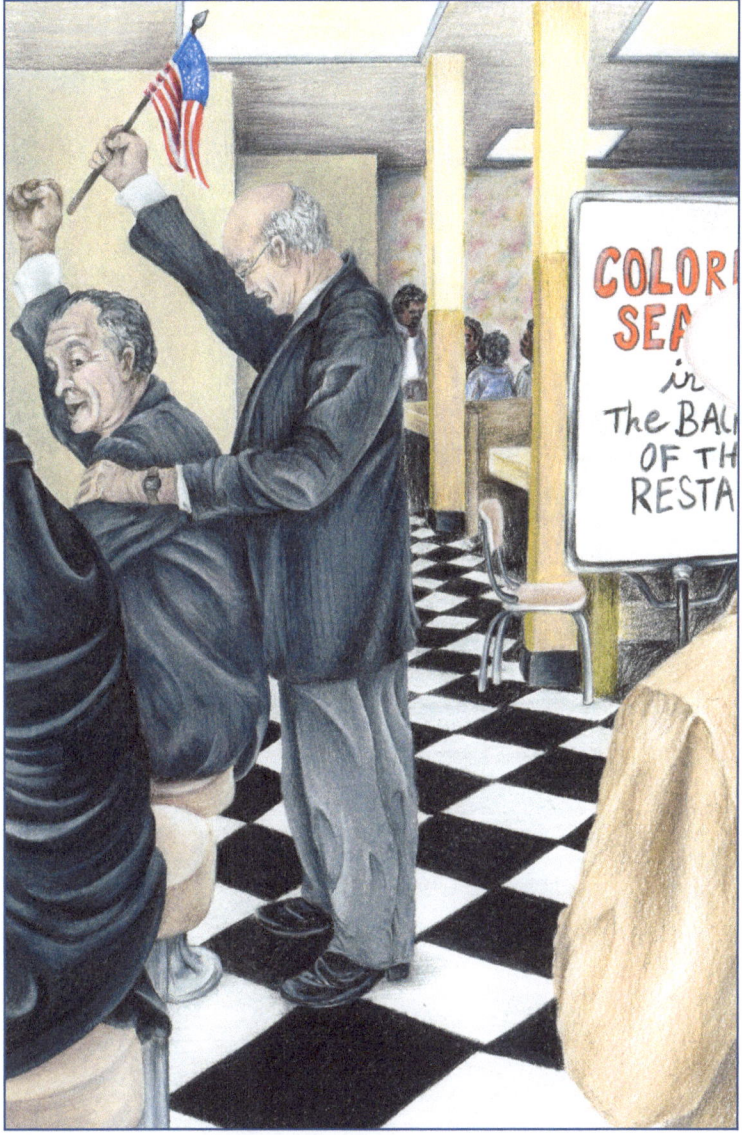

We don't think that we should have to sit around and wait for some segregationist congressmen and senators and a President from Texas in Washington, D.C., to make up their minds that our people are due now civil rights. No, we want it now or we don't think anybody should have it.

Supplementary Information

- Malcolm X re-emphasizes what he sees as the hypocrisy of American leaders who keep delaying justice and equal rights for blacks.
- Malcolm X questioned the sincerity of President Lyndon Johnson, saying, "the President is from a cracker state. ... They'll hang you quicker in Texas than they will in Mississippi. Don't you ever think that just because a cracker becomes president he ceases being a cracker."

- Malcolm X gave examples of what needed to happen. In order to have peace and security for African Americans, "we have to eliminate the barking of the police dogs, we have to eliminate the police clubs, we have to eliminate the water hoses, we have to eliminate all of these things that have become so characteristic of the American so-called dream. These have to be eliminated. Then we will be living in a condition of peace and security."

Comprehension and Discussion Questions

- What does segregationist mean? *People who supported the forced separation of the races.*

- Why do you think Malcolm X says he doesn't think African Americans should have to wait for leaders to decide to "give" them civil rights? *Answers will vary.*

- What do you think Malcolm X means by his last sentence? *The last sentence could be taken as a threat, and once again shows Malcolm X's willingness to use violent means to achieve his goals.*

Notes: _____
_____
_____
_____
_____
_____
_____
_____
_____

Supplementary Information

- Malcolm X explained, "When we say Afro-American, we include everyone in the Western Hemisphere of African descent. South America is America. Central America is America. South America has many people in it of African descent. And everyone in South America of African descent is an Afro-American. Everyone in the Caribbean, whether it's the West Indies or Cuba or Mexico, if they have African blood, they are Afro-Americans. If they're in Canada and they have African blood, they're Afro-Americans. If they're in Alaska, though they might call themselves Eskimos, if they have African blood, they're Afro-Americans."

Comprehension and Discussion Questions

- Who does Malcolm X hope to unite in the OAAU? *All people of African heritage in the Western Hemisphere.*

- What do you think Malcolm X means by "unite"? *Get them to put aside their differences and work toward a common goal.*

- Malcolm X gave this speech after leaving the Nation of Islam, a group that limited membership only to Muslims. How does Malcolm X broaden his mission with the OAAU? *He is not seeking to unite only Muslims, but all African-American peoples, regardless of religion.*

Notes: _____

_____

_____

_____

So the purpose of the Organization of Afro-American Unity is to unite everyone in the Western Hemisphere of African descent into one united force. And then, we will unite with our brothers on the motherland, on the continent of Africa.

We must unite together in order to go forward together.

Supplementary Information

- Malcolm X especially wanted to emulate the way the OAU had brought together individuals and groups with very different backgrounds and objectives. "Those who formed the organization of African states have differences. They represent probably every segment, every type of thinking. You have some leaders that are considered Uncle Toms, some leaders who are considered very militant. But even the militant African leaders were able to sit down at the same table with African leaders whom they considered to be Toms. ... They forgot their differences for the sole purpose of bringing benefits to the whole."

- Malcolm X urged his audience to take matters into their own hands when the justice system in America failed them. "Tactics based solely on morality can only succeed when you are dealing with people who are moral or a system that is moral. A man or system which oppresses a man because of his color is not moral. It is the duty of every Afro-American person and every Afro-American community throughout this country to protect its people against mass murderers, against bombers, against lynchers, against floggers, against brutalizers and against exploiters."

Comprehension and Discussion Questions

- What does Malcolm X say that African Americans must do in order to go forward? *They must unite.*

- What are some ways you yourself unite with others into a group in order to help the group as a whole? *Students may suggest playing on a sports team, acting in a school play, working on group projects in class, or standing up for members of their family.*

- Malcolm X believed that most white Americans of his time did not think of themselves as American, even if they were born in the United States. Do you think that is true today? *Answers will vary.*

Supplementary Information

- Malcolm X insisted the OAAU remain under the control of African Americans. No whites could join the OAAU. Further, no donations from whites would be accepted.
- Tensions increased between Malcolm X and the Nation of Islam in 1964.
- Malcolm X was killed while addressing an OAAU rally in 1965. He was shot by a member of the Nation of Islam.

Comprehension and Discussion Questions

- How does Malcolm X compare Africa to America? *They are linked; one cannot go forward faster than the other.*
- Malcolm X thought nonviolent protests (like marches and boycotts) would not change an unjust system. Do you agree? *Answers will vary.*
- Malcolm X called for African-American parents to withdraw their children from white schools until schools employed black principals, black teachers, and used textbooks written by black people. Do you think this was a good idea? Why or why not? *Answers will vary.*
- Malcolm X's ideas are sometimes called "Black Nationalism." Can you think of any reasons why this might be? *Answers will vary.*

Notes: _____
_____
_____
_____
_____

Africa will not go forward any faster than we will and we will not go forward any faster than Africa will. We have one destiny and we've had one past.

_____
_____
_____
_____
_____

Malcolm X's OAAU Founding Rally Address

We have formed an organization known as the Organization of Afro-American Unity.

We want freedom by any means necessary.
We want justice by any means necessary.
We want equality by any means necessary.

We don't think that we should have to sit around and wait for some segregationist congressmen and senators and a President from Texas in Washington, D.C., to make up their minds that our people are due now some degree of civil rights.

No, we want it now or we don't think anybody should have it.

When we say Afro-American, we include everyone in the Western Hemisphere of African descent.

So the purpose of the Organization of Afro-American Unity is to unite everyone in the Western Hemisphere of African descent into one united force. And then, we will unite with our brothers on the motherland, on the continent of Africa.

We must unite together in order to go forward together. Africa will not go forward any faster than we will and we will not go forward any faster than Africa will.
We have one destiny and we've had one past.

Name: _____ Date: _____

Wrap-up Discussion Questions

- What kind of person does Malcolm X seem to be? Would he make a good friend, or older brother?

- What does Malcolm X seem to be trying to make his audience feel? Do you think he did a good job?

- What questions would you want to ask Malcolm X if you had been present at his OAAU address?

- Do you think race should be what unites people? If not, what should it be?

- Think of two ancient proverbs: 1) "An eye for an eye, a tooth for a tooth," and 2) "Turn the other cheek." Which one would Malcolm X agree with?

- How would you compare this speech to one given by Martin Luther King Jr.?

- Malcolm X said his group wanted equality by any means necessary. What is good about this approach? What might be bad about it?

- If he were alive, what do you think Malcolm X would think about America today?

Teaching Suggestions

Activity I: Close Reading

Separate the class into pairs or trios and give each group a slip with an excerpt from *Malcolm X's OAAU Founding Rally Address* (**Graphic Organizer A**). Have them put the sentence(s) in their own words. After a few moments, reconvene the class and distribute complete copies of **Handout A** to each student. Have groups read their paraphrases in turn, and discuss each as a class and decide if it is a faithful and complete paraphrase. Have students complete the chart on **Handout A** with the class paraphrases. When all slips are completed, read the original version of *Malcolm X's OAAU Founding Rally Address* aloud and discuss how the class version compared with the original.

Activity II: Journaling

Have students interview their older family members or grandparents about what life was like in America during the 1960s. If the family did not live in the United States during this time, students should talk to neighbors and other people in their communities. Encourage them to ask about the Civil Rights Movement specifically. Did any family members face discrimination? Did any participate in demonstrations? Have students reflect on what they learned in a one-page journal entry.

Activity III: Compare and Contrast

After reading the OAAU address, have students fill out one side of a Venn diagram with key words, phrases, and images from Malcolm X's speech. Then have students watch a video of Martin Luther King's *"I Have a Dream"* address. Next have them complete the Venn diagram. Videos can be found at http://www.thekingcenter.org/.

Activity IV: Application

Have students complete **Handout B: Attitude Inventory** independently. Discuss each statement as a large group and invite students to share their responses. Then have them write a response to Malcolm X, explaining whether and why they agree or disagree with him. Letters should be about one page in length.

Name: _____ Date: _____

Graphic Organizer A

We have formed an organization known as the Organization of Afro-American Unity.	*Put this passage in your own words:*
We want freedom by any means necessary.	*Put this passage in your own words:*
We want justice by any means necessary. We want equality by any means necessary.	*Put this passage in your own words:*
We don't think that we should have to sit around and wait for some segregationist congressmen and senators and a President from Texas in Washington, D.C., to make up their minds that our people are due now some degree of civil rights. No, we want it now or we don't think anybody should have it.	*Put this passage in your own words:*
When we say Afro-American, we include everyone in the Western Hemisphere of African descent. So the purpose of the Organization of Afro-American Unity is to unite everyone in the Western Hemisphere of African descent into one united force. And then, we will unite with our brothers on the motherland, on the continent of Africa.	*Put this passage in your own words:*
We must unite together in order to go forward together.	*Put this passage in your own words:*
Africa will not go forward any faster than we will and we will not go forward any faster than Africa will. We have one destiny and we've had one past.	*Put this passage in your own words:*

Name: _____   Date: _____

Handout B: Attitude Inventory

Directions: *Read the following ideas, which are all taken from Malcolm X's OAAU address. Mark each statement with an "A" for agree or a "D" for disagree. Be ready to talk about your reasons with your classmates:*

1. Everyone has the right to defend him/herself. _____

2. Only black teachers know the best way to teach black children. _____

3. Be nonviolent only with those who are nonviolent to you. _____

4. If you have a dog, I must have a dog. If you have a rifle, I must have a rifle. If you have a club, I must have a club. This is equality. _____

5. When the government can't or won't protect people, the people should protect themselves by whatever means necessary. _____

President Reagan's Speech on the Challenger Disaster

Today is a day for mourning and remembering. Nancy and I are pained to the core by the tragedy of the shuttle Challenger. We know we share this pain with all of the people of our country. This is truly a national loss.

We've grown used to wonders in this century. It's hard to dazzle us. But for twenty-five years the United States space program has been doing just that. We've grown used to the idea of space, and perhaps we forget that we're only just begun. We're still pioneers. They, the members of the Challenger crew, were pioneers.

The future doesn't belong to the fainthearted; it belongs to the brave. The crew of the space shuttle Challenger honored us by the manner in which they lived their lives. We will never forget them, nor the last time we saw them, this morning, as they prepared for the journey and waved goodbye and "slipped the surly bonds of earth" to "touch the face of God."

Note to Teacher on Context:

President Reagan's speech began: "Ladies and gentlemen, I'd planned to speak to you tonight to report on the State of the Union, but the events of earlier today have led me to change those plans ... "

Notes: _____

Introduction

Ronald Reagan

Late in the morning on January 28, 1986, the space shuttle Challenger lifted off from Kennedy Space Center in Florida. It was a very special event because a schoolteacher was part of the crew and would be going into space. The event was televised and people everywhere — including schoolchildren in classrooms across the country — were watching.

Just more than a minute into its flight, something terrible happened. The shuttle broke apart in a cloud of smoke. People everywhere were shocked and saddened.

President Ronald Reagan had been planning to give his yearly State of the Union address that night. But he decided it was more important to talk to his fellow citizens about the Challenger disaster. President Reagan gave a speech that evening in which he expressed his sorrow for the loss of the seven brave people aboard the Challenger. He also praised the daring and heroic ways they had lived their lives.

What Is a Primary Source?

A primary source is a piece of history. It is an artifact from a time period, like a diary, a speech, a newspaper article, or a photograph. In this chapter, you will study *President Reagan's Challenger Disaster Address* as a primary source from 1986, as a way to learn about that time period of American history.

Activating Prior Knowledge: Questions for Pre-Reading Discussion

1. Have you ever watched the space shuttle take off or land?
2. Have you watched news reports about the International Space Station?
3. What do you know about the Challenger shuttle disaster?
4. Why do you think President Reagan decided to make a speech to the country on the day of the Challenger disaster?
5. The name of the shuttle that exploded was the Challenger. What does that word make you think of?
6. What challenges have you faced in your own life? What challenges does your class take on? Your city? Your country?

Vocabulary and Context Questions

Complete this page as you read. Using context clues and/or a dictionary, define each word:

Vocabulary

challenge: *a difficult but often enjoyable task*

mourning: *grieving, feeling sad for a loss*

tragedy: *a very sad event*

wonders: *amazing things*

pioneer: *the first one to go into a territory or to do something*

surly: *threatening, difficult to deal with*

bonds: *chains or shackles*

Context Questions

1. Who delivered this speech? *President Ronald Reagan*

2. When was it written? *1986*

3. What was its purpose? *To comfort and lead the nation after the Challenger disaster*

4. Who listened to this speech? *American citizens and people all over the world who watched on television*

Supplementary Information

- The seven astronauts who died in the Challenger explosion were Michael Smith, Dick Scobee, Judith Resnik, Ronald McNair, Ellison Onizuka, Gregory Jarvis, and Christa McAuliffe.
- *President Reagan's Challenger Disaster Address* was written by Peggy Noonan.
- President Reagan began his speech by saying he had planned to give the State of the Union address that night, but the events of the day had led him to change his plans.

Comprehension and Discussion Questions

- How does President Reagan say the day should be spent? *Mourning and remembering — or grieving for those who died and thinking about what they did.*
- Who do you think Nancy is? *President Reagan's wife.*
- What is a challenge? *A new task or activity that will be hard to do.*
- Why do you think NASA decided to name the shuttle the Challenger? *Answers will vary.*
- President Reagan began his speech by saying he had planned to give the State of the Union address that night, but the events of the day had led him to change his plans. Why do you think he made this decision? Was it the right choice? *Answers will vary.*

Notes: _____
_____
_____
_____

Today is a day for mourning and remembering.
Nancy and I are pained to the core by the tragedy of the shuttle Challenger.
We know we share this pain with all of the people of our country.

_____
_____
_____
_____

This is truly a national loss.

Comprehension and Discussion Questions

- What does Reagan mean by "national loss"? *The whole country feels the pain of the disaster; the space program belongs to everyone.*
- How do you think people felt when they watched on television as the shuttle exploded, or learned of the disaster later? *Answers will vary, but may include sad, scared, or angry.*

Notes: _____

_____
_____
_____
_____
_____
_____
_____
_____
_____
_____
_____
_____
_____
_____
_____
_____
_____
_____
_____
_____
_____
_____

Supplementary Information

- In 1967, three NASA astronauts were killed during a launch simulation test when their spacecraft caught fire on the launch pad.
- As of 1986, the United States space program had never lost an astronaut *in* space.

Supplementary Information

- The U.S. space program began with the Mercury missions in 1959.
- The first American in space, Alan Shepard, flew on Freedom 7 in 1961.
- The first American to orbit the Earth, John Glenn, flew on Friendship 7 in 1962.
- Astronauts Neil Armstrong and Buzz Aldrin became the first men to walk on the moon in 1969. Additional moon missions continued until 1972.
- The space shuttle program was started in 1972 and the first shuttle, the Columbia, was launched in 1981.

Comprehension and Discussion Questions

- What does Reagan say the U.S. space program has been doing for 25 years? *"Dazzling us" or performing amazing feats of science, engineering, and bravery.*
- What qualities did NASA engineers show as far back as 1959? What about NASA astronauts? *Answers may include initiative, perseverance, bravery, courage and determination.*
- What do you think Reagan means when he says Americans have "grown used to wonders"? *We've been seeing the space program perform amazing feats so often that we forget that what we are watching are, in fact, amazing feats. The "miracles" have become common, and we have taken for granted, or forgotten, that there is real danger involved.*

We've grown used to wonders in this century. It's hard to dazzle us. But for twenty-five years the United States space program has been doing just that. We've grown used to the idea of space, and perhaps we forget that we've only just begun.

Notes: _____

_____

_____

_____

We're still pioneers.
They, the members of the Challenger crew, were pioneers.

Supplementary Information

- The American pioneers traveled with their families, pushing the American frontier west. They often suffered hardships and illnesses, and many died during their travels into the unknown.

- Three days after the Challenger disaster, President Reagan gave a eulogy for the crew. He said, "We think back to the pioneers of an earlier century, and the sturdy souls who took their families and their belongings and set out into the frontier of the American West. Often, they met with terrible hardship. Along the Oregon Trail you can still see the grave markers of those who fell on the way. But grief only steeled them to the journey ahead.

Comprehension and Discussion Questions

- What do you think of when you hear the word "pioneers"? *Answers will vary, but may include covered wagons, families moving westward, the Gold Rush, the Oregon Trail.*

- What did the crew of the Challenger (and all astronauts) have in common with the pioneers? *They pushed the boundaries of what was known or understood. The pioneers traveled and settled into unknown lands, and the astronauts ventured into what some have called the final frontier — space. As President Reagan himself said, "Today, the frontier is space and the boundaries of human knowledge."*

Notes: _____

Supplementary Information

- In another part of his eulogy, President Reagan expanded on the idea that the future is secured by and belongs to the brave: "We learned again that this America, which Abraham Lincoln called the last best hope of man on Earth, was built on heroism and noble sacrifice. It was built by men and women like our seven star voyagers, who answered a call beyond duty, who gave more than was expected or required, and who gave it with little thought to worldly reward."

Comprehension and Discussion Questions

- To whom does Reagan say the future belongs? *The brave.*

- Who does Reagan say the future does not belong to? *The fainthearted — or those who are too timid or fearful to take on new challenges.*

- Do you agree with what Reagan says about brave people and the future? *Answers will vary.*

- How do individuals like those who served on the Challenger crew capture the future? *By taking risks to push the boundaries of new knowledge. This can lead to new scientific discoveries, new understandings, and new adventures for mankind.*

Notes: _____

_____

_____

_____

_____

_____

The future doesn't belong to the fainthearted; it belongs to the brave.

_____

_____

_____

_____

_____

The crew of the space shuttle Challenger honored us by the manner in which they lived their lives.

Supplementary Information

- In his eulogy for the crew, President Reagan said the United States would not stop the space program because of the tragedy. He said family members of the fallen crew had all told him that their loved one would have wanted the program, to which they had dedicated their lives, to continue.

- President Reagan also said, "Man will continue his conquest of space. To reach out for new goals and ever greater achievements — that is the way we shall commemorate our seven Challenger heroes."

- President Reagan appointed a special commission to investigate the cause of the accident. The shuttle program came to a halt for 32 months while the commission looked for answers.

- It was discovered that an "O-ring" seal failure had caused the disaster and that there were serious flaws in NASA's communications and decision-making processes.

Comprehension and Discussion Questions

- When President Reagan says the crew honored "us," who does he mean? Who is "us"? *The American people.*

- What was the manner in which the Challenger astronauts lived their lives? *Fearlessly, courageously, with determination and with a sense of duty to something greater than themselves.*

- How can you personally live your life courageously? *Answers will vary.*

- Who do you honor when you do that? *Answers will vary but may include oneself, family members, friends, loved ones, teachers, coaches, community members, God.*

Notes: _____

_____

_____

_____

_____

_____

Supplementary Information

- The quoted lines are taken from a poem called "High Flight," written by Pilot Officer John Gillespie Magee Jr. in 1941.
- Pilot Officer Magee died during World War II.

Comprehension and Discussion Questions

- How does President Reagan describe the last time we saw the Challenger crew? *That morning, waving goodbye as they prepared for their flight.*

- President Reagan quotes a pilot who was also a poet in these last lines of his speech. How does the poet compare the Earth to the sky? Which does the poet prefer? *The Earth is something to which the pilot is bonded or chained. When he is flying, he is able to free himself from the bonds of Earth and enter a heavenly realm. The pilot prefers the sky.*

- Why do you think President Reagan selected this poem to quote in his speech about the Challenger disaster? *The lines tell of a pilot's love for the sky, and the inspiration of flying. [The poet also died in the air.] The pilot and the Challenger astronauts all died doing what they loved.*

Notes: _____

We will never forget them,
nor the last time we saw them, this morning,
as they prepared for the journey and waved goodbye
and "slipped the surly bonds of earth" to "touch the face of God."

President Reagan's Challenger Disaster Address

Today is a day for mourning and remembering.

Nancy and I are pained to the core by the tragedy of the shuttle Challenger.

We know we share this pain with all of the people of our country.

This is truly a national loss.

We've grown used to wonders in this century. It's hard to dazzle us.

But for twenty-five years the United States space program has been doing just that.

We've grown used to the idea of space, and perhaps we forget that we've only just begun.

We're still pioneers. They, the members of the Challenger crew, were pioneers.

The future doesn't belong to the fainthearted; it belongs to the brave.

The crew of the space shuttle Challenger honored us by the manner in which they lived their lives.

We will never forget them, nor the last time we saw them, this morning, as they prepared for the journey and waved goodbye and "slipped the surly bonds of earth" to "touch the face of God."

Name: _____ Date: _____

Wrap-up Discussion Questions

- Do you think Americans found President Reagan's speech comforting?

- How does President Reagan feel about the Challenger astronauts?

- What does President Reagan want the American people to feel about their deaths?

- What personal qualities does President Reagan believe the astronauts demonstrated?

- Seven people died in the Challenger disaster, which is a small number compared with the number of people who die every day (in car accidents, for example). Why did President Reagan address the nation about this event, when he does not address the nation if seven people die in a horrible car accident?

- After the Challenger astronauts died, some thought the United States should shut down the space program. Does President Reagan believe that is what the astronauts would have wanted? How do you know?

- The space shuttle Columbia disintegrated on re-entry in 2003. Do you remember that day? Have your parents or other family members ever talked about it?

Teaching Suggestions

Activity I: Close Reading

Separate the class into pairs or trios and give each group a slip with an excerpt from *President Reagan's Challenger Disaster Address* (**Graphic Organizer A**). Have them put the sentence(s) in their own words. After a few moments, reconvene the class and distribute complete copies of **Handout A** to each student. Have groups read their paraphrases in turn, and discuss each as a class and decide if it is a faithful and complete paraphrase. Have students complete the chart on **Handout A** with the class paraphrases. When all slips are completed, read the original version of *President Reagan's Challenger Disaster Address* aloud and discuss how the class version compared with the original.

Activity II: Compare and Contrast

Discuss with students the idea that the Challenger astronauts were pioneers. Ask them to brainstorm qualities shared by American pioneers and the Challenger crew, along with the shared qualities of the Western frontier, and the qualities of space. Use **Handout B** as a guide.

Activity III: Creative Writing

Have students imagine they are part of a nomination committee to suggest individuals who should be in a Citizenship Hall of Fame. What would they say about any of the members of the Challenger's crew? Ask them to select a crew member, spend some time researching their life, and then write a three- to five-minute nomination speech to a Citizenship Hall of Fame.

Activity IV: Application

Ask students to recall the last lines of "High Flight" quoted by President Reagan in his address. Then ask them to think of a place they personally like to go — a place that makes them feel happy and free. Have them write a ten-line poem in which they contrast their special place with their usual surroundings. Encourage them to use the style from the original poem in their closing line, "slip the _____ of _____ to _____."

Name: _____ Date: _____

Graphic Organizer A

Today is a day for mourning and remembering. Nancy and I are pained to the core by the tragedy of the shuttle Challenger. We know we share this pain with all of the people of our country.	Put this passage in your own words:
This is truly a national loss.	Put this passage in your own words:
We've grown used to wonders in this century. It's hard to dazzle us. But for twenty-five years the United States space program has been doing just that. We've grown used to the idea of space, and perhaps we forget that we've only just begun.	Put this passage in your own words:
We're still pioneers. They, the members of the Challenger crew, were pioneers.	Put this passage in your own words:
The future doesn't belong to the fainthearted; it belongs to the brave.	Put this passage in your own words:
The crew of the space shuttle Challenger honored us by the manner in which they lived their lives.	Put this passage in your own words:
We will never forget them, nor the last time we saw them, this morning, as they prepared for the journey and waved goodbye and "slipped the surly bonds of earth" to "touch the face of God."	Put this passage in your own words:

Name: _____ Date: _____

Handout B: Pioneers

Qualities of pioneers	Qualities of astronauts
Qualities of the Western frontier	Qualities of space as a "frontier"

Write a sentence summarizing why President Reagan compared the Challenger astronauts to pioneers.

About the Author

After teaching for seven years, Veronica Burchard became the Director of Curriculum Development for an educational nonprofit organization near Washington, D.C. She earned her bachelor's and master's degrees in English from the University of Florida, and her interests include American literature and civic education. Veronica lives with her husband, two sons and a very hungry guinea pig in Fairfax, Virginia.

www.ingramcontent.com/pod-product-compliance
Lightning Source LLC
Chambersburg PA
CBHW040054160426
43192CB00002B/71